i

A TRANSFORMATION FROM A MIND OF POVERTY TO A MASTER OF POETRY

A TRANSFORMATION FROM A MIND OF POVERTY TO A MASTER OF POETRY

A EYE OPENING JOURNEY OF SPIRITUAL REDIRECTION CASTING THE TRUE REFLECTION OF BEAUTY IN A INDIVIDUAL

POETRY BY LACRECIA LESLEY

ISBN 978-0-578-51579-3 (Paperback}

Library of Congress Control Number 2019907728

Cover image by Lacrecia Lesley

Published by Cre8tions Plus Publications

11220 West Rd

Houston Tx 77065

This book is dedicated to my heavenly father whom changed my life. Also a special dedication to all of the families who will see and receive the message in the poetry. Life is so full of trials and error, but love seems to always forgive.

Table of Contents

INTRODUCTION

My name is Lacrecia Lesley, at a certain time in my life you couldn't have told me that I would be able to step outside of myself, meaning mind ,body and soul and self-diagnose an image of myself. I was once told that I needed to take a long look in the mirror, but even the reflection of myself was quite deceiving. The person I truly am was so well hidden behind the captivity of fear and uncertainty. Who would have thought that an individual could be held captive inside ones own mind to the extreme of losing your identity. Well welcome to my world. The imaginary world that I built inside of my mind in order to feel accepted. I recreated my own image. I guess you could say that I lost my spiritual connection, but my connection spiritually didn't lose me. I was dying inside of this wonderful body the Lord created. It was not until I stepped outside of my mind, and body from my delusional perspective, so I could be saved by a gift hidden beyond my blinding true image of myself, Information placed inside of me as a guide or a road map to my freedom. Welcome to my world, a true introduction to my life, my words, my poetry.

PEACE

I could have been a shadow but there was no one in front to follow.

They could have saved our lives but instead their hearts were hollow

We should have been family built strong within a legacy of kings

But instead we are all separated and wrapped up in to worldly things

I'm about to share my spiritual experience of what it is to fall from grace

How I stepped out from behind the shadow and in life I found my place

You cannot live a life of fear and prosper with the gifts from above

Deny yourself or the people around you the nourishment of respect and love

So come and take a walk with me I'm letting you inside my space

I will show you the damage fear and uncertainty can do to the human race

As I share my life filled journey from the pages of my book

Depleting the memories from a created image and a totally new outlook

So welcome to my world, my introduction and new release

Of how I found the true I am and through him I found peace

KIND WORDS

To know me is to connect with an innocent stranger

I have not a warning for a friend but a few preventions from danger

Kind words is what I offer to a heart that is pure and true

Your inner most personality is what opens my eyes to you

I am different unlike any individual that you will ever meet

The cure for a peace of mind is the formula for defeat

A true friend can show you the success within yourself

In order to make progress there will be no hazards to your health

Try and understand that my heart is in your favor

Each day that you have a problem your task becomes my labor

My thoughts of you are constant my mind continuously run astray

Follow the pattern which is planned for you and be led every step of the way

Close your eyes to the confusion and let the darkness be unheard

As I reveal to you the tree of life in this message of kind words

SHADES OF BLUE

As I live each day in this troubled world where there are hearts made of stone

Different shades and colors to go through my mind and tell a story that could never be known

If I could reach in my heart and remove a color it would be a distinctive shade of gold

A sign of life for every young child of God and the grace of being able to grow old

A drifting leaf from a tree can be a serious sign of loneliness sadness and depression

Because life itself is full of shades of green meaning money is my brother's obsession

The explanation of the colors white and black has been the destruction of God's world

Because in the beginning there wasn't a shade or a color, only the distinction between boy and girl

If man or woman could have reached deep in their souls and found that person my Lord once knew

There would have never been the colors white or black only beautiful shades of blue

CRUSHING PETALS

Where is a loving heart as the world comes to an end.

What happened to the trust and peace from the lips of a close friend

Are we lost completely trapped in a zone of hatred and deceit?

Divide by the faces of death on the material created from a tree.

How lost indeed can a person be to the wisdom of receiving a blessing?

What kind of message are you sending to an innocent mind whom thrives for a good impression?

How long will we walk in the path of violence in fear of a unreasonable death?

 What soul in this world has the power of decision to cancel another souls breath?

Can we continue our journey with peace and joy receiving life's rewarding medals?

 Remove the sword from the hands of the unkind feet who are continuously crushing petals

A HISTORY OF SHADOWS

I cast a shadow from a faraway place.

 Memories of my ancestors mothers of a strong race

I stand tall among the soil and buried beneath my feet.

Shows the images of many fathers cast from limbs of oak trees.

I am strong within my hands, and carry a smile throughout my pain.

I am the strength carried through my off spring and the sun which follows the rain

I stood strong behind the brother who fought to carry our name

I stood stiff among the faces whom tried to put my family to shame

I am a history of images cast down throughout the years

I am the undertaker of bad news my closet withholds many tears

Throughout my life I shall provide, determination, strength from a nation, and through God my salvation

Many books have held the description of the journey along my path

The length of my troubles and the road blocks I have had

But I am still here and continue to stand strong

I have carried my life and the life of my young

Who I am do you ask? I am the black woman I stand proud and free as a sparrow

I am a image of mothers, the strength behind brothers, I am a history of shadows

A INNOCENT MIND

As I watch the small features of those timid creatures visions go through my mind

Taking to the extreme the most beautiful things a complete breakthrough for all mankind

Bright lights dance through their eyes and harmony moves through their voices expressing their ideas and distorted thoughts

Yet no one ever listens to that small star that glistens now ask yourself who is to fault?

The pitter patter of little feet and that once muttered heartbeat fades away slowly with time

Giving every bit of a God filled lesson teaching you to love, the utmost blessing and the strength coming from an innocent mind

MOLDED SOULS

Deep in pit of a cold and possessed mind

Lies a thought of deception and extended amount of crime

Expressed with anger and repeated abuse of the heart

Not digging deep enough to cope with the fears from the start

The walls are deteriorating and your feet begin to pause.

My life is at a dropping point from a dreadful abnormal cause

I am idol my mind is blank and filled with horrifying terror

My eyes are closed with a seal of an uneducated error

Wake up cries a voice filled with knowledge and delight

It's not too late to stand up straight cross the path and do
what's right

Open me up and fill your head with the power of what I hold

Release me from the shelves of the dusty molded souls

CHANGE

As I awake in the morning with a level of ambition

A life changing experience to encourage a strong mission

Staggering throughout the years with the thought of success

Failure to coordinate my steps lead to a creative mess

A voice of innovative motives leading me into a direction

The words filter into my thoughts like an organized collection

My destiny was never lost, it was simply put on hold

Time wasted can cost and procrastination gets old

Pushing forward to completion is the key to unlock the door

Raising the belief levels in oneself will leave you wanting more

In order to achieve success your thoughts will rearrange

No longer an unorganized mess and your life will begin to change

COLOR

The concept of identifying with an object of descriptive matter

Creating difference of opinion do to diverse chatter

The art to discover admiration in the beauty of nature

A priceless image subjected to this worlds cruel waiver

The love available to an individual is pure bliss and anew

Completely hidden beyond distinction as I spoke of in Shades of Blue

There are no two alike in which separates the one from the chain

A reaction created in a form of deception in which one should refrain.

Walk your mile in the shoes you choose to complete the distance of no other

Live your dreams beyond the reflection of a world confused by the simplicity of color

I USED TO

I used to worry, I used to get in a hurry, but what did it matter? What did it help?

It was simply a hazard to my health

Now I spread my time between sunrises and sunsets

A compromise to the wise until my needs are met

I stumble no more between the fine lines , because now I write the rhythm of my beat in which moves my feet

A tempo that uplifts my eyes to the center of my focus

The miracles being performed unclear to a world of hocus pocus

Seeing my father as not a magician, understanding can collectively remove the superstition

I search the soul for nourishment and wisdom

No longer a prisoner to a programmed system

I dive deep within the thoughts of a profound creation

A destined being existing among an entire nation

I am creative and I think no more about, way back then, or what could have been

Now I think about the things I can do⋯And never to reminisce again about what I used to

SKIN

Lets reverse the universal curse brain washed so you can't win.

The one that said, you weren't good enough because of your gender or skin

Your reflection does not determined your worth, nor reveals your gift inside

You have been brain washed since the moment of birth and told by the world to hide

The truth is beauty has no reflection it is only felt not seen

You have to seek the wisdom of God to understand just what I mean

To reflect goes deeper than the surface of sight it travels to the depth of one's mine.

Redirect your energy to the beauty inside before the negative robs you of your time

If you are trying to find yourself within a reflection you are chasing petals in the wind

The truth is reflection does not cast an image it lies beneath the surface of one's skin

WINDING DOWN

I'm winding down and can see my reflection

The words were the freedom and Gods perfection

Falling from grace and become my protection

They slowed down my pace and changed my direction

Now its time, the rain no longer shadow my tears

I'm done carrying dead weight dragging my feet through the years

I won this race how do I call myself a winner?

I changed up my life and consumed the word of God for dinner

I can see my face my reflection has improved

I deleted the social media and the bullying was removed

I am beautiful as far as the eye can see

I am still here because God revealed my reflection to me

People cannot control you, they can only talk and form an opinion

They did not mold you in their attempt to establish Dominion

Can you hear me when I say that your life has meaning?

Come be near me when you're afraid my God hears you screaming

Children stand strong through the evil that lurks through town

I promise it wont be long your victory is winding down

MYSTERIOUS SHADOW

I feel the presence of a spirit lingering ever so near

Guiding my life into curious directions making everything so clear

I am not afraid of your guidance for you possess what I need

You are light of living the love of giving the fruit in which I greed

Awaken me at night my spirit from the coma of despair

Touch me and enhance my feelings making me fully aware

Embrace me with the thought of success before my clock comes to a halt

Release this enormous amount of pressure in which puts each individual to fault

Bless me my friend as my time comes to an end to fly away as free as a sparrow

For when life pays you a visit you don't want to miss it, it lurks behind a mysterious shadow

MY SELFLESS REFLECTION

Look into my eyes can you see what is hurting me?

If it takes you by surprise see how damaging words can be?

I was told I wasn't good enough to be a human being

Between the mean looks and all the harsh words I couldn't believe what my eyes were seeing

I cant explain how it made me feel my reflection will never be the same

Close my eyes wishing this day was not real for merely existing I felt so ashamed

Go through life and carelessly breaking all the rules, continuously crushing another person's dreams

If I could lift my head and sing a song, it would yes my Jesus loves me

For all the times these people did me wrong his love would set me free

I will continue on singing Jesus love song his love is my resurrection

He helped me to see the true value in me and through faith my selfless reflection

GIFTED

I cant breathe sometimes the air gets thick

My mind is processing my thoughts so quick

I have sleepless nights as my words will scatter

I awake to find out that nothing is the matter

I challenge my thoughts throughout the day where I speak

I process it all as my mind is on repeat

The voice of the subconscious will send signals of what I heard

But unless my father directs my mind I refuse to utter a word

I am an author and finisher waiting to make my debut

Because you are reading my work my calling has come true

The meaning of my purpose is to empower and be uplifted

It is a blessing from the Lord to be anointed and gifted

BROKEN SMILES

As I walk out in the sunlight and embrace the rays of warmth against my skin

I realize the blessings to inhale once more as my face has the comfort of the wind

As I move forward each day in time, I watch my footsteps blaze trails

My life in the hands of my master the gift of wisdom has a story to tell

My heart celebrates the words of repair, my feet dance with excitement for people everywhere

The truth will share endless life among the earth for millions of miles

There will be no more sadness, only freedom from worry, and no more broken smiles

SWEET SUCCESS

Comfortable and free is my mind at last

Swaying through the memories of my imaginable past

Frozen in my steps as I whisper sweet melodies

What is this peace that I've captured inside of me

As I express with my lips and glide with my pen

I whisper words from a stranger to a unknown friend

Welcoming you to my world captured in a thought

Releasing a priceless treasure beyond being bought

Safe is a child educated by wisdom

Invisible is this heart to life's cruel prison

Dance with my mind on the edge of complete sanity

Brushing the dust from your eyes from a

crystal clear vanity

My objectives indeed require less confusion

My world as a positive and all negatives an illusion

I will continue my journey with grace and finesse

Living comfortable in the arms of my sweet success

A WALK ON THE OTHER SIDE

The true knowledge of life a peaceful sleep

The journey between realms where the church will meet

The return of our king instruments of song will shatter

 The truth only will be told and nothing else will matter

Praises will raise and shout as the world will surely end

Heads will bow to the king as the true life will begin

The truth was in the word as spiritual prophets would
continuously teach

But death bound many ears as these words weren't able to
reach

The word is of Gods love as his love will always prevail

In the beginning was Gods love as his love will never fail

Gods light shines in the blind as the path is dimly lit

Faith will seal your eyelids as your soul becomes legit

This is a message to the righteousness that the truth will always reside

In the hearts of his children who are willing to put away the pride

I am the messenger of my maker in remembrance of the souls whom died

I have come to regain the new souls life for a walk on the other side

MISTY CONDITIONS

Caught in a storm of blissful thoughts

The rain was not upon my parade, but yet the mind was at fault

I tried to sparkle between dreams, only to find my smiles were incomplete

I've traveled many miles within these streets, determined to stay on my feet

I am bold beyond the definition that is found within a glossary

The strength comes with the wisdom you seek

This book could never be the definition of me

I am a woman set out to accomplish and complete a very strong and determined mission

Weathered the storm in the comfort of my makers arms, despite the cause of the misty conditions

HERE I AM

I have captured a rainbow of images beautiful faces by far

Traveled many miles in my mind, by plane, on a bus, and in my car

Dreamed many years, through restless nights

Awaken to these thoughts grasping my memories so tight

I could see the entire family that was intended to be

Stretched beyond millions of miles just waiting for me

Gods grace has provided us with will and strength

A miraculous reunion full of glorifying intent

Breaking through all barriers like the force of a ram

I have awaken to my destiny, hello world here I am

NEVER TO TURN BACK

I am writing for he that is in me

The love that set me free

The grace which warmed my heart

And gifted me from the start

Roamed across many hills and plains

Wondering if my steps were insane

The rain would come and wash away the tears

Love would remove the doubt for the new years

I am swept off of my feet by the visions instead

The whispers of a new life writing my steps ahead

Where there is love there are no failures your path is clear

The awakening will embrace you as your success is near

Free to live peacefully with a life that is on track

Guided by our heavenly father and never to turn back

PRECIOUS LOVE

As I sit here in my thoughts frozen in my steps I wept

Mother you are the breath I breathe I was a soul you conceived and safely kept

I pray every day for your sunrises and sunsets, full moons to illuminate the room in the bed where you slept

My soldier, my queen, who would stand by me in all situations

A strong woman of all nations, the laborer of all relations

Come and pray with me mama in my spirit where you will always be

Where you will hear my heart of every countless hour beat

I long for your touch, mama I love you so much

Can I pull back that cloud and shout this out loud

To my mother I am proud!...to be your son, your job here was perfectly done

This race you have won

In my house, you have only just begun, to spread your memories the distance between the moon and the sun

I will carry your memories in my heart with every step I take

Praise God for all of the years that I could see your face when I awake

You are as strong as a sparrow, and as gentle as a dove

Rest in peace my sweet mother, my dear, my precious love

A MESSAGE TO DELIVER

Its morning time and Gods glory sweeps across the earth

As his messenger awaits for his children's return and rebirth

Blessed is the man who carries out his instructions

Saved are the souls who were once fearful and reluctant

How great is he that places the gift of love on man's pure heart

Precious is the rib who has stood by his side through faith from the start

Today we celebrate the two whom have multiplied by one

Formed by a higher power, the creator of the moon and the sun

As we continue this journey along this life's predestined path

Living without the promise of how long this life will last

I will raise him up praise him and fall upon my knees

We have become the family we are today because it was our God whom you have pleased

There is a time to teach, and a time to pray, a time to rejoice in every second of the day

A time to love as our blood flows like a river

A precious time to release a message to deliver

NOT OUR PLAN

When my father calls, I will always embrace his hand

In the comfort of his glory, with wisdom I will stand

You were the light that awakened me in my time of need

A guide among the pathways for a soul to succeed

My eyes began to focus and my heart became pure

My faith became stronger with every passing year

As my life began to lift beyond this spiritual plain

So many friends will be missed as Jesus has called my name

The memories of our unity will continue throughout the days

Due to the strength of our families, whom taught us our ways

To our God we will praise when called to take a stand

As we are numbered in our days and our lives are not our plan

ANGEL

I met an Angel so full of love

With the presence of peace from her God above

She brought me smiles each time we would explore

Sharing moments are so pleasant with this Angel I adore

Life is so precious connecting paths for us to meet

A night filled journey with stories before she sleeps

Each time when we separate I pray her days are full of joy

Each moment she shares her wisdom I'm like a child with a brand new toy

I have met many wonderful people throughout this journey in my life

Which makes me continue to move forward and never to think twice

You are a blessing to your family the proof that love will never fail

To fly high beneath the wings of such a beautiful angel

PIANO MAN

To dream the vision of keys, notes pressing the sound of beauty beneath your finger tips

Beats that make your heart trip, rhythm to make the heart skip

I found a man with a talent and he created a perspective

His notes where a collaboration of a collective

He saw the music lost within my voice

He brought the song back and gave life a new choice

I can see between the years that were lost to your recognition

I would like to acknowledge my admiration of you if that's ok? with your permission

You are the hope that I dreamed, the person that seemed impossible to exist

Through the eye glass of the world the dynamic was missed

You invited my eyes spiritually to gaze and begin again

Open the doors to a higher power for two souls to win

You are my hero don't you know?

You brought back the beauty which makes Gods love show

I didn't sign up for a class I signed up for forever

Taking down obstacles that makes a whole world better

We are a force whom will conquer and complete Gods plan

I am the sound beneath the notes of my piano man

MELODY

The power of song, this piece won't take me long

Notes created to give sound, so let me break this down

Tapping feet in the street, every sound owns a beat

Ears are ringing all around, the musicians talent is pound for pound

There is power in this instrument

To perfect this song there were hours spent

If you listen long enough you might feel these vibes

Oh this rhythm is so bold, the music is changing lives

Let me slow down,

Did you hear that hook? Between the piano and the man playing bass

The music is so smooth, the musician had a grove, everybody had a smile on their face

The instructor said, let me break this down, so we can perfect this song

The art of music is so profound, this piece won't take me long

I just wanted to share this moment of what the art and music can do

While you're sitting there listening and tapping your feet the next musician can be you

If you took the time to read this poem may the talent in you be set free

Instead of sitting and listening to someone else song, step up and create your own melody

YOU ARE THE BEST

A queen meant to sit on her throne

Strong to operate on her own

Able to withstand the pressures of the world

Survived the torments from the age of a little girl

Brown is her skin of sheer radiance I adore

Her company is of educated moments and keeps you wanting more

Who is she do you ask? She is the strength traveled through history

Aging bones and crumbling thrones through our eyes there is no mystery

Come with me my queen who have traveled here through time

Endured the turmoil's of your life and through blessings have given me mine

Who is this queen do you ask? She is the sister to all of the brothers

But from my aspect, she kept my life in check, this queen just happens to be my mother

You gave me comfort when I had fear, told me God was here and your prayers laid all things to rest

You are my queen beyond all things, the life in which God brings me to describe to the world that Mother⋯You are the Best!

SPECIAL THANKS

To my mother for believing in me and seeing the vision.

To my children with lots of love

To my uncle, thank you for all of your support

Visit my website at

www.cre8tionspluspub.com

GOD BLESS

www.ingramcontent.com/pod-product-compliance
Lightning Source LLC
Chambersburg PA
CBHW061524050726
47503CB00016B/2737